こどものためのピアノ曲集
# 風のプレリュード
新実徳英：作曲

The piano pieces for CHILDREN for small hands
## Preludes of Winds
composed by Tokuhide Niimi

カワイ出版

この曲集のCDは、
ビクターエンタテインメント株式会社より発売中です。

The CD is available from
VICTOR ENTERTAINMENT.

[ ビクターエンタテインメント：VICS-61217
風のプレリュード
こどものためのピアノ曲集
演奏：高橋多佳子 ]

[ VICTOR, [No.VICS-61217]
PRELUDES OF WINDS
The piano pieces for CHILDREN
for small hands
Pianist : Takako Takahashi ]

---

**皆様へのお願い**

楽譜や歌詞・音楽書などの出版物を権利者に無断で複製（コピー）することは、著作権の侵害（私的利用など特別な場合を除く）にあたり、著作権法により罰せられます。また、出版物からの不法なコピーが行われますと、出版社は正常な出版活動が困難となり、ついには皆様方が必要とされるものも出版できなくなります。
音楽出版社と日本音楽著作権協会（JASRAC）は、著作者の権利を守り、なおいっそう優れた作品の出版普及に全力をあげて努力してまいります。どうか不法コピーの防止に、皆様方のご協力をお願い申しあげます。

カワイ出版
一般社団法人　日本音楽著作権協会

# はじめに

〈風のプレリュード〉全12曲がやっと上梓のはこびとなりました。というのは、３年も前に依頼を受けたのに、なかなか書き始めることができず、1990年の秋にやっと糸口をつかみ1991年の８月まで少しずつ書き溜め完成したものだからです。

「世界中を旅する風が、いろんな土地で聴いた旋律や歌を僕のところへ運んでくれる、僕はそれらに耳を傾け、共感し、そして記憶に残った断片をもう一度鍵盤の上で組み立て直す」、つまり、いわば〈私〉を捨てたところから作曲を始めようと考えたのでした。

結果、でき上がった曲たちを眺めていると、やはり〈私〉はそこにいますし、その濃淡も様ざまなのですが、これまでの曲にいる〈私〉とは随分異なるように思えます。

そのことがこの曲集全体に、まさに風の透明感と同時にその確かな存在感を与えてくれているとすれば、私の考え方は間違いではなかったといえましょう。

曲は技術的に非常に易しいものからやや難しいものまで、およそ順に並べてありますが、順にやっていく必要は全くありません。うんと乱暴に言えば、弾きたい曲からやっていけば良いとすら私は思っています。

実は６曲でき上がったところで初演をしていただいたのですが、これは大人が弾き大人が聴くのにも十分に耐えられるとの評判もいただきました。いろんなところで、いろんなやり方でこの曲集をとり上げて下されば作曲家冥利に尽きるというものです。

最後に、この貴重な機会を与えて下さったカワイ出版とそのスタッフの方がた、とりわけ編集の服部一夫さんには多大な御苦労をおかけしました。ここに心からの謝意を表するものです。また一部初演を快よくお引き受け下さった瑤の会(田中瑤子主宰)の皆さん(伊芸悦子、嘉手納弘美、金井美雪、佐竹優子、時志京華、仲宗根聡子)——このことがなかったら完成はもっと遅れたに違いありません——にも心から御礼申し上げます。

新実徳英

(東京・東中野にて、1992年３月)

# Preface

"Preludes of Winds" complete in twelve pieces has finally reached the stage of publication, for I could not easily make a start though I had been asked to write as long as three years before, and it was in the fall of 1990 that I found a clue at long last, then I have worked with them little by little and by one all through the year until the August of 1991 to see them finally completed.

The clue is "The winds travelling all around the world will bring to me various melodies and songs that they hear in various places. I will listen to them, sympathize with them, and construct those fragments retained in my memory all over again on the keyboard." In other words, I just wanted to make a start after I gave up 'myself'.

Consequently, I still found 'myself' there in all tints when I saw those pieces completed, but quite different from the previous 'myself' in the previous pieces.

If the collection as a whole could bring about a certain feel of existence as well as of transparency of the wind at the same time, then it would go to prove that my idea was not wrong.

The pieces are put in order as a general rule according to relative difficulty in technique, from the easiest to fairy hard, but it does not at all need to learn them in its order. In a loose sense of the word I think you can just begin with whatever you like to play.

Six of them had already been premiered as soon as they were finished, and that they are good enough for adults' performance and appreciation. I hope this collection would be put to use in many occasions in many ways, which is one of those things that make me thankful to God for being a composer.

In conclusion let me express my gratitude to Edition KAWAI and the staff, who gave me this valuable opportunity, especially to Mr. Kazuo Hattori, editor in chief. And I would also like to thank the members of Yo no kai(under the presidency of Yoko Tanaka), Etsuko Igei, Hiromi Kadena, Miyuki Kanai, Yuko Satake, Kyoka Tokishi, and Satoko Nakasone, who readily accepted the premiere of part of the collection. Were it not for their cooperation would be much behind. Here I offer my heartfelt thanks to them all.

**Tokuhide Niimi**

in Higashinakano, Tokyo

March 1992

# も　く　じ／CONTENTS

1. 風 踊っている
Winds...Are Dancing ——————————————————— (ca. 1′10″) ——————— page 6

2. 銀色の風
Silver Wind ——————————————————— (ca. 1′40″) ——————— 10

3. 不気味な風が……
There Comes an Ominous Wind ——————————————————— (ca. 1′10″) ——————— 13

4. シシリアの風
Sicilian Wind ——————————————————— (ca. 1′50″) ——————— 16

5. 風のノクチュルヌ
Nocturne of Winds ——————————————————— (ca. 3′10″) ——————— 19

6. ウィンド イン ブルー
Winds in Blue ——————————————————— (ca. 2′00″) ——————— 22

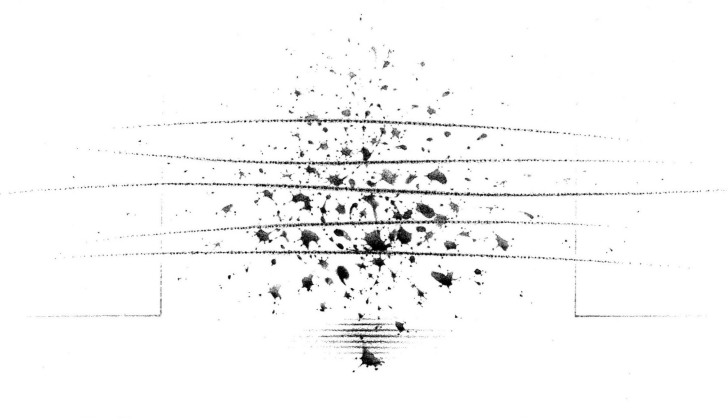

| | 演奏時間 | page |
|---|---|---|
| 7. 風は想う<br>The Wind Muses... | (ca. 2′05″) | 26 |
| 8. 西風のつぶやき<br>Mutter of the West Wind | (ca. 2′10″) | 28 |
| 9. アンダルシアの赤い風<br>Red Wind from Andalusia | (ca. 2′00″) | 31 |
| 10. トロピカル ウィンド<br>Tropical Wind | (ca. 3′50″) | 39 |
| 11. 風の悲しみ =ドビュッシーへのオマージュ=<br>Winds in Sorrow —an Homage to Debussy— | (ca. 5′00″) | 44 |
| 12. 風は見る……<br>The Wind Sees... | (ca. 5′05″) | 54 |

各曲の演奏時間は参考のためにのみ記してあります。

# 1

## 風 踊っている
### Winds... Are Dancing

拍子は〔4/4拍子＋3/4拍子＋2/4拍子＋3/4拍子＋3/4拍子〕の五小節単位でできています。
軽やかな変拍子の舞曲。
右手と左手でリズムを刻みつつ、旋律が浮かび上がるように弾きましょう。

The time pattern is composed of <4/4+3/4+2/4+3/4+3/4>, five measures as a unit.
This is a light dance music in irregular time.
Just play so that the melody comes up in front with the right and the left hand beating the rhythm.

新実徳英　作曲
Tokuhide Niimi

© Copyright 1992 by edition KAWAI, Tokyo, Japan.
International Copyright Secured, All Rights Reserved.

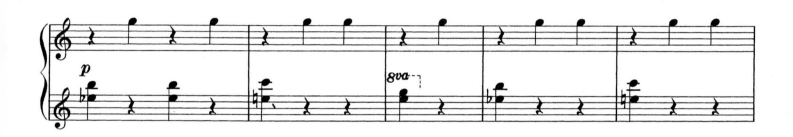
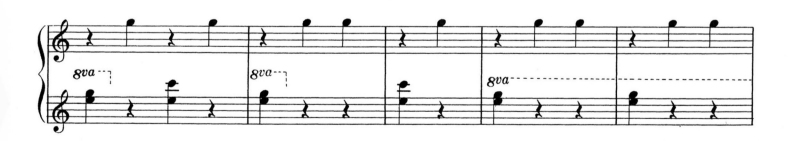

# 2
## 銀色の風
### Silver Wind

月の光に照らされた雪の野原を銀色の風がしめやかに吹き抜けていきます。
♩♪ はあまり弾まないように、しずかに、ひたひたと。

A silver wind gently blows through a snow field lit by the moonlight.
♩♪ should not be too bouncing but quiet and placid.

新実徳英　作曲
Tokuhide Niimi

© Copyright 1992 by edition KAWAI, Tokyo, Japan.
International Copyright Secured, All Rights Reserved.

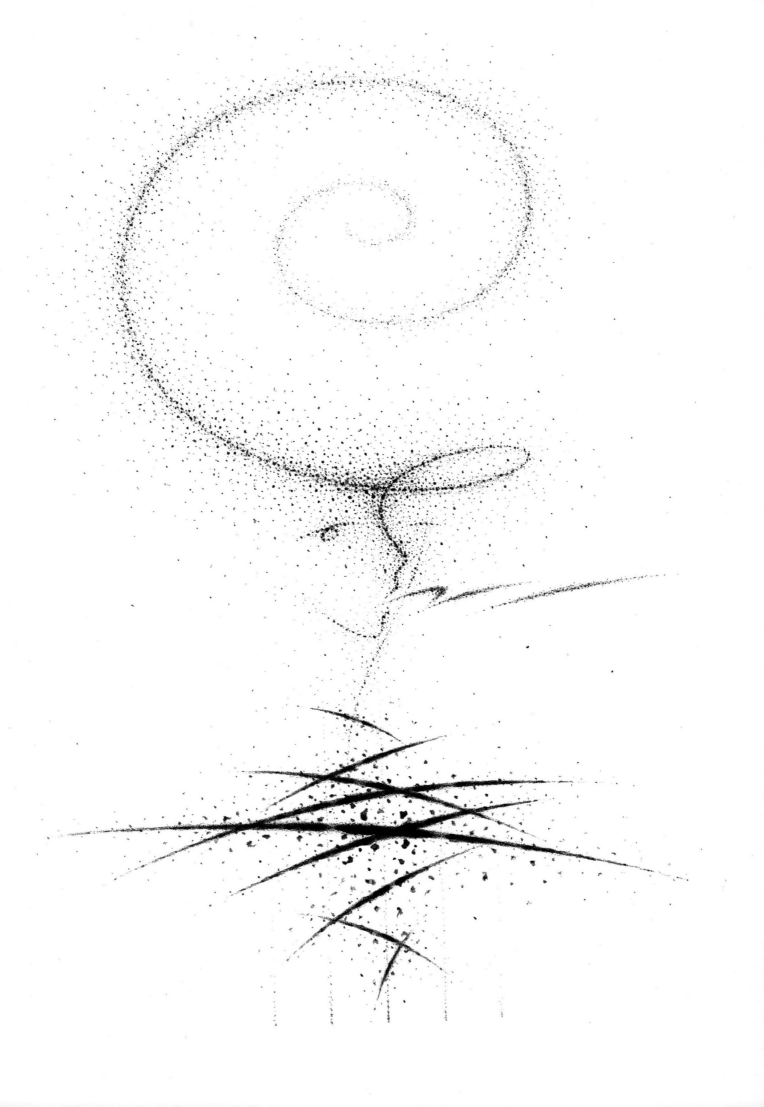

# 3
## 不気味な風が……
### There Comes an Ominous Wind

暗闇の奥から不気味な風が……。やがて大きな渦となって吹き荒れるのです。
テンポは速いのですが、♩♩♩ や ♩♩♩♩ の音型が前のめりにならないように。

There comes an ominous wind from the deep darkness....and then it howls frightfully in big whirls.
The tempo should be fast but note that the figures like ♩♩♩ and ♩♩♩♩ do not lean forward.

新実徳英　作曲
Tokuhide Niimi

*¹ 5/8拍子の全体を一拍として感じるように。
(2/8拍子＋3/8拍子ほどではなく。)
Feel the whole 5/8 time as one beat, not as ⟨2/8 time ＋ 3/8 time⟩.

*² ∥はゲネラル・パウゼで。以下同様に。
Generalpause, similarly.

© Copyright 1992 by edition KAWAI, Tokyo, Japan.
International Copyright Secured, All Rights Reserved.

14

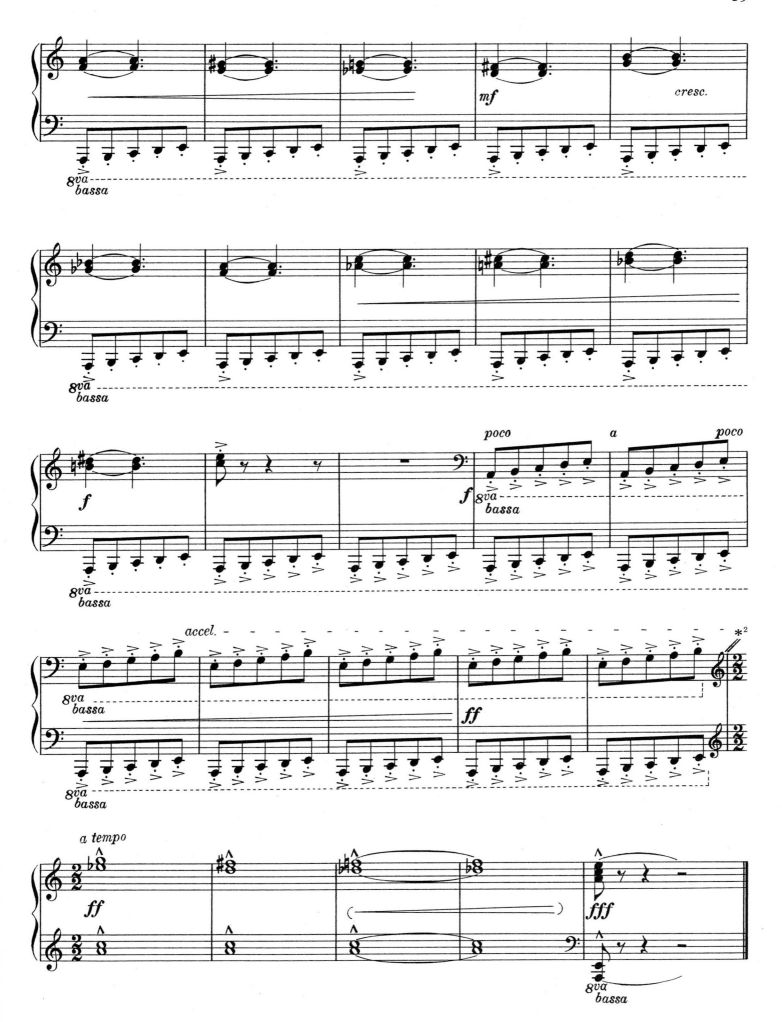

# 4
# シシリアの風
## Sicilian Wind

いわゆるシシリアーノ（シシリア風舞曲）の一種です。
古くはJ.S.バッハに、新しくはG.フォーレにもありますから是非聴いてみて下さい。
♩♪ のしなやかなリズム感、6/8拍子の流れを大切に。

This is a kind of siciliano, a Sicilian dance music.
You can find more of this kind, of older in J.S.Bach's and of newer in G.Faure's. I strongry advise
you to listen to some of them.
Take care of the flexibility and rhythmic feel of ♩♪ and the line in 6/8 time.

新実徳英　作曲
Tokuhide Niimi

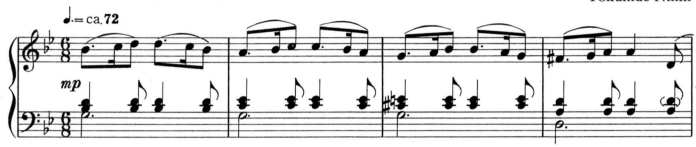

© Copyright 1992 by edition KAWAI, Tokyo, Japan.
International Copyright Secured, All Rights Reserved.

# 5
## 風のノクチュルヌ
### Nocturne of Winds

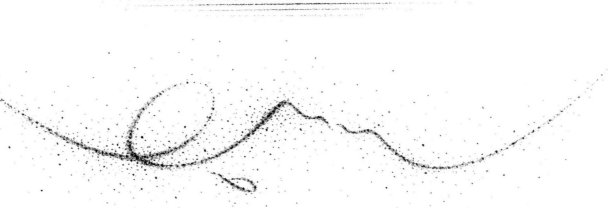

優しく暖かな風のノクターン。
やわらかくふくらみのある音色を心がけて下さい。ヴィブラフォーンのイメージ。
前奏部分のペダリングに注意。音が順に混ざっていくように。

This is a nocturne of a gentle and mild wind.
Here is needed a soft and swelling tone color. Just imagine that of the vibraphone.
Be careful of the pedalling of the introduction, so that each note is blended in one by one.

新実徳英　作曲
Tokuhide Niimi

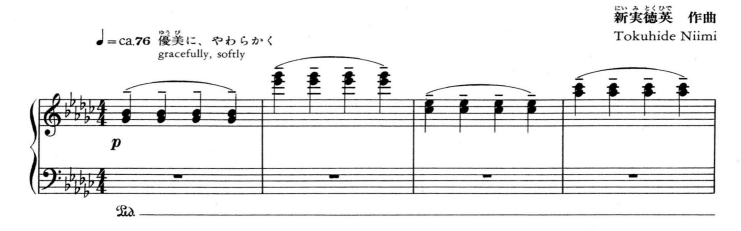

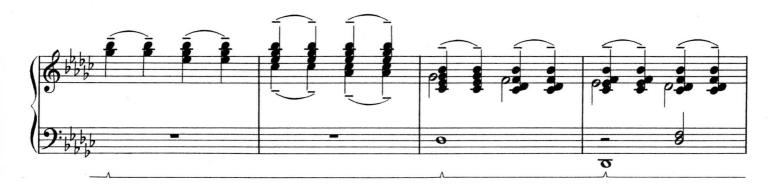

© Copyright 1992 by edition KAWAI, Tokyo, Japan.
International Copyright Secured, All Rights Reserved.

# 6
## ウィンド イン ブルー
### Winds in Blue

元気の良い?! ブルース。
クラシックしか勉強したことのない人はこの機にガーシュインなど聴いてみて下さい。
この曲の感じがつかみ易くなると思います。
3連音符のリズムのノリ、流れを大切に。

Cheerful(?!) blues.
If you have studied solely classics, take this opportunity to try and listen to Gershwin's and that will help you get at the essence of this piece.
Make much of the feeling and the line in triplet rhythm.

新実徳英 作曲
Tokuhide Niimi

♩=144 はぎれよく、リズムにのって
in a clear tone, on the beat to the rhythm

© Copyright 1992 by edition KAWAI, Tokyo, Japan.
International Copyright Secured, All Rights Reserved.

# 7
# 風は想う
## The Wind Muses....

この曲集の中で一番表現の難しい曲かもしれません。
反復されるFの音、それをとりかこむ様ざまな和音がFの音に表情の起伏をつけていきます。
和音の変化を鋭敏に感じとって下さい。

This might be the most difficult in expression among the collection.
Repetition of F, surrounded and modified by various chords, gradually puts on an expressive look with colorful emotions.
Be acute enough to feel the changes in chords.

新実徳英 作曲
Tokuhide Niimi

♪=ca.72 感情の起伏を大切に
Make much of the colorful emotions.

© Copyright 1992 by edition KAWAI, Tokyo, Japan.
International Copyright Secured, All Rights Reserved.

# 8
## 西風のつぶやき
### Mutter of the West Wind

西ヨーロッパ風の旋法、のイメージで作られた曲。
透明なハーモニー、くっきりとした、それでいてやわらかな旋律を浮き出させて下さい。
 のところは全音と半音が交互になっている旋法でできています。

Based on the image of the West European mode.
Remember to outline the transparent harmony and the clear but soft melody.
In  is adopted the mode of alternation of whole tones and semitones.

新実徳英 作曲
Tokuhide Niimi

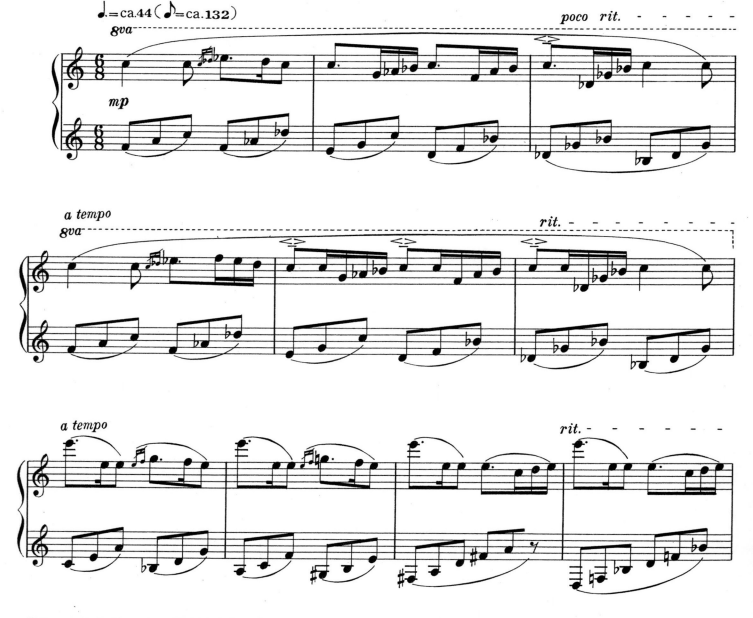

© Copyright 1992 by edition KAWAI, Tokyo, Japan.
International Copyright Secured, All Rights Reserved.

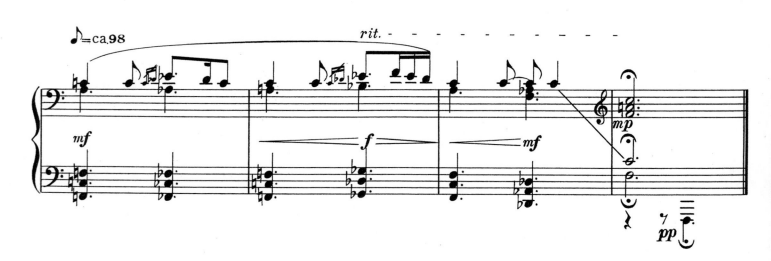

# 9
## アンダルシアの赤い風
### Red Wind from Andalusia

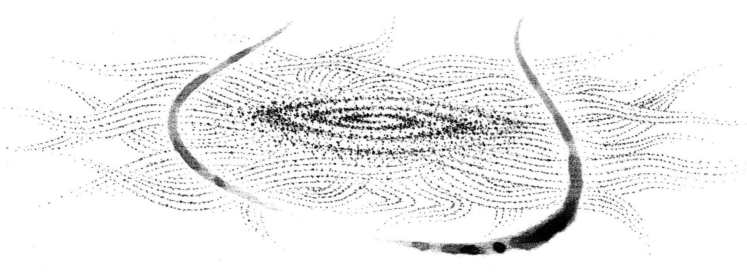

スペイン風の激しい舞曲です。
途中で『カルメン』の一節がチラリと顔を出します。
二種類のテンポ（**Tempo I**と**Tempo II**）をはっきりと区別して下さい。

This is a Spanish dance full of passion.
A phrase from "Carmen" makes a slight appearance in the middle of the piece.
Be sure to recognize the distinction between different tempos (Tempo I and Tempo II).

新実徳英　作曲
Tokuhide Niimi

© Copyright 1992 by edition KAWAI, Tokyo, Japan.
International Copyright Secured, All Rights Reserved.

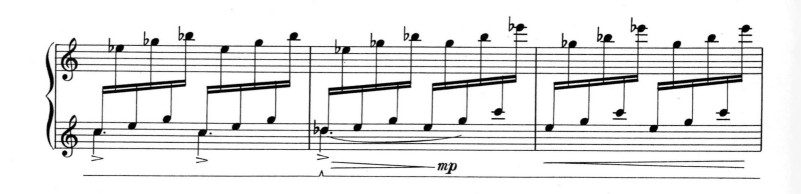

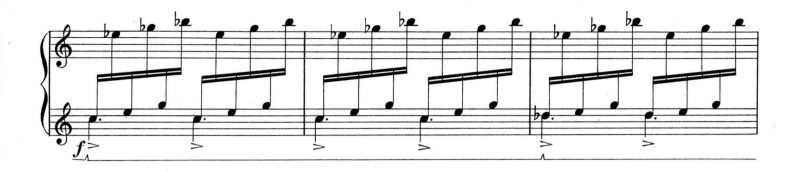
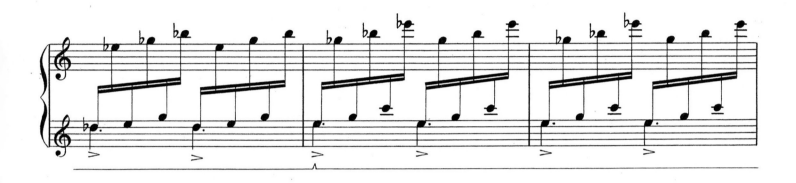
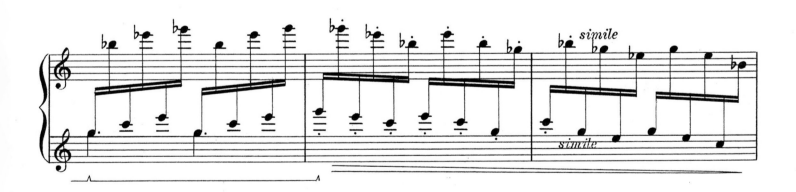

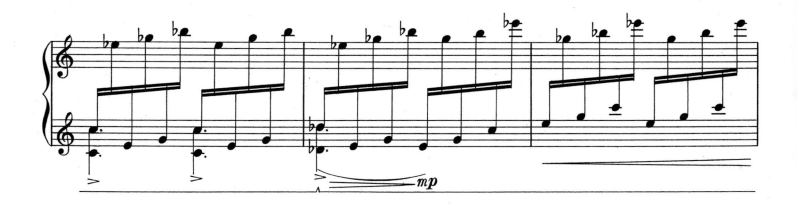
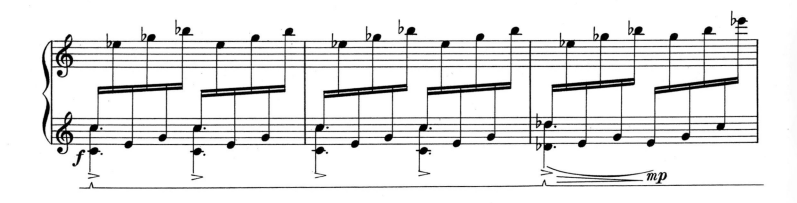

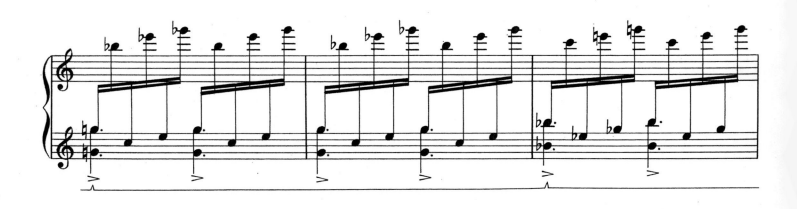

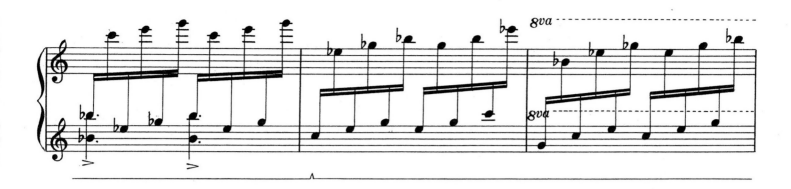
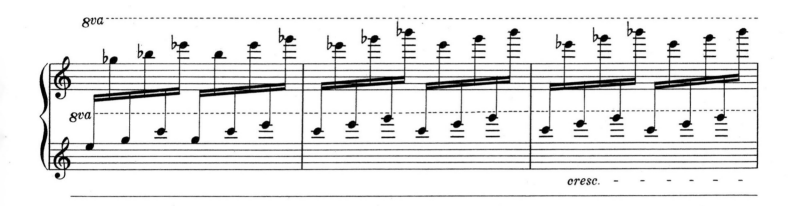
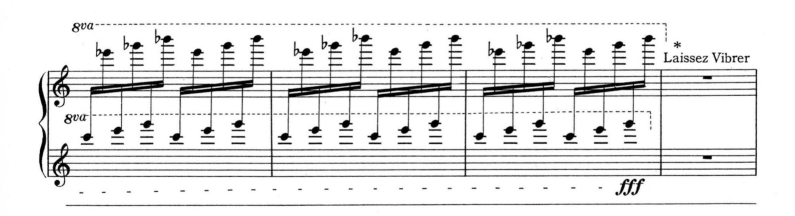
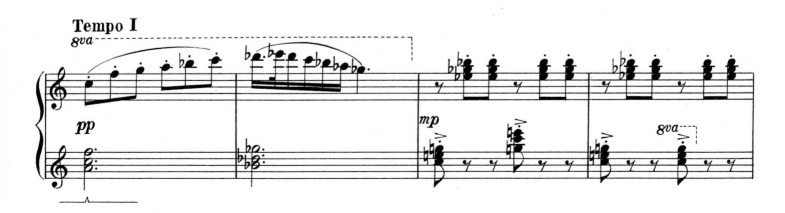

*Laissez Vibrer（仏語）は、余韻をよく響かせて。

36

**Tempo II**

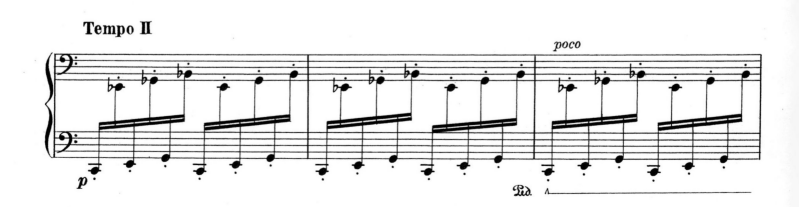

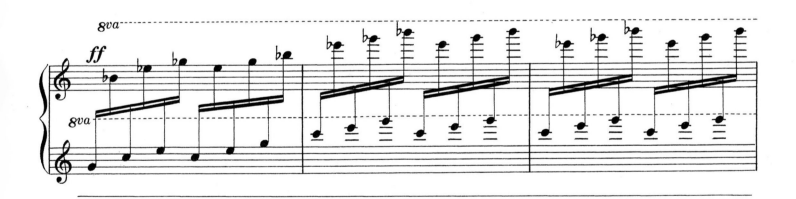
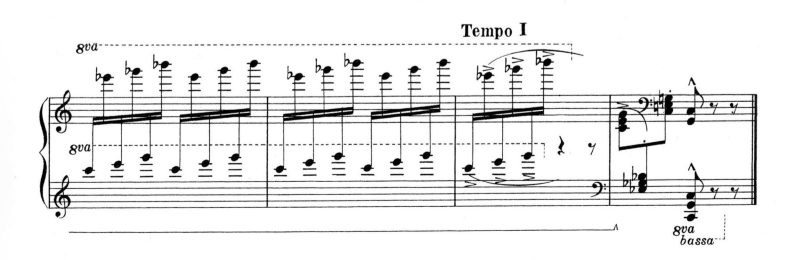

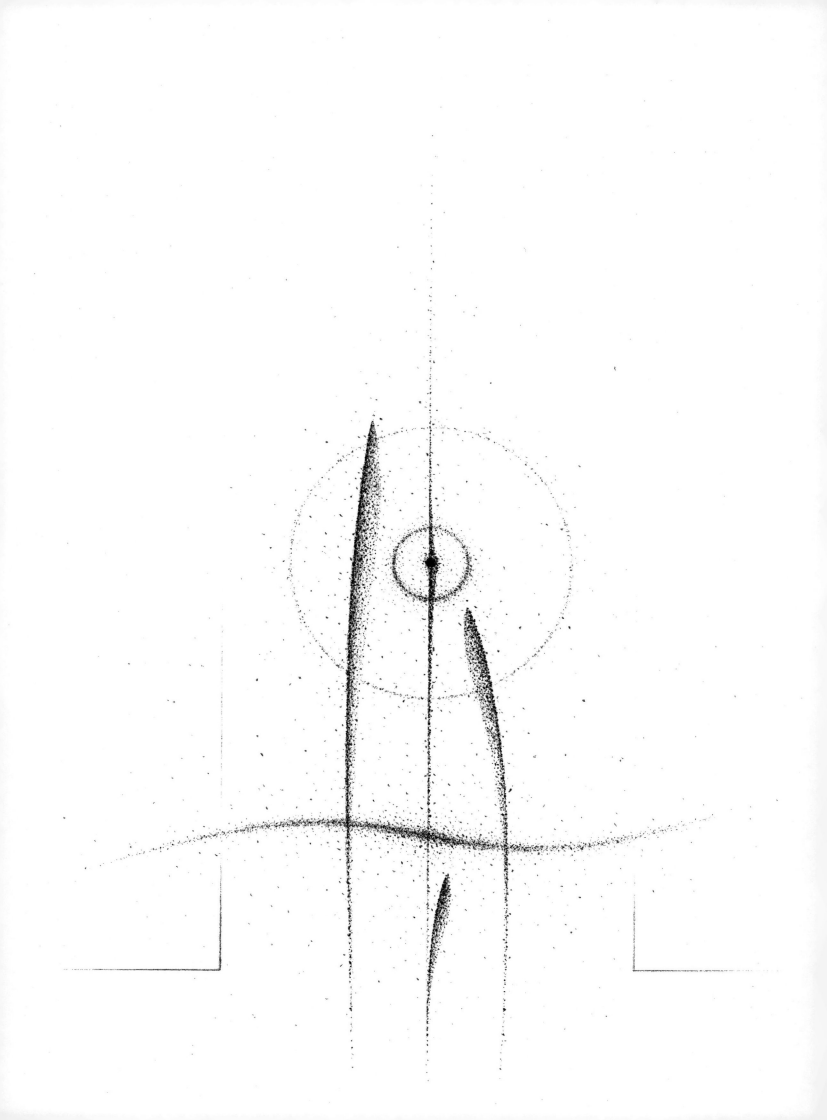

# 10
# トロピカル ウィンド
## Tropical Wind

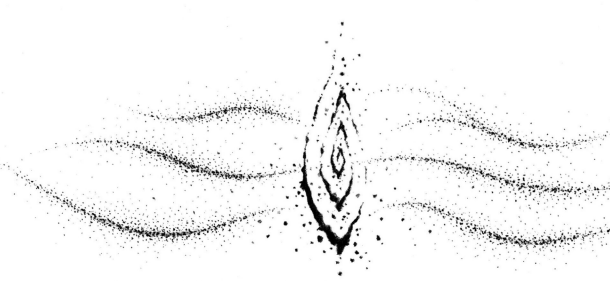

インド、インドネシアに特有の旋法で作られています。
ガムラン風アッチェレランドもでてきます。
冒頭は 𝅘𝅥𝅮𝅘𝅥𝅮𝅘𝅥𝅮𝅘𝅥𝅮 を素早く弾き、♩の音だけを残します。
♩=72の箇所からのペダルは音がにごり過ぎない程度に踏みかえていって下さい。

Here is used the characteristic mode of India and Indonesia, including accelerando like gamelan.
At the beginning, play 𝅘𝅥𝅮𝅘𝅥𝅮𝅘𝅥𝅮𝅘𝅥𝅮 very quickly and leave the note of ♩ only behind.
Shift the pedalling properly on the part of ♩=72 so as not to make the sound mixed up to excess.

新実徳英 作曲
Tokuhide Niimi

♩=60 もの憂く、熱く
gloomily, hot

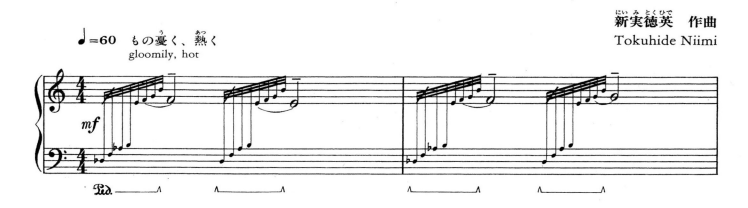

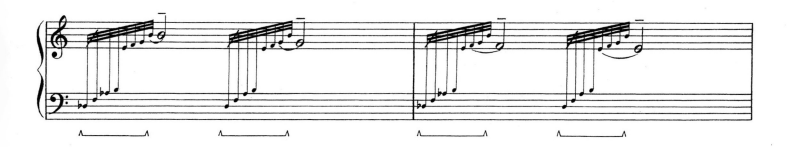

© Copyright 1992 by edition KAWAI, Tokyo, Japan.
International Copyright Secured, All Rights Reserved.

42

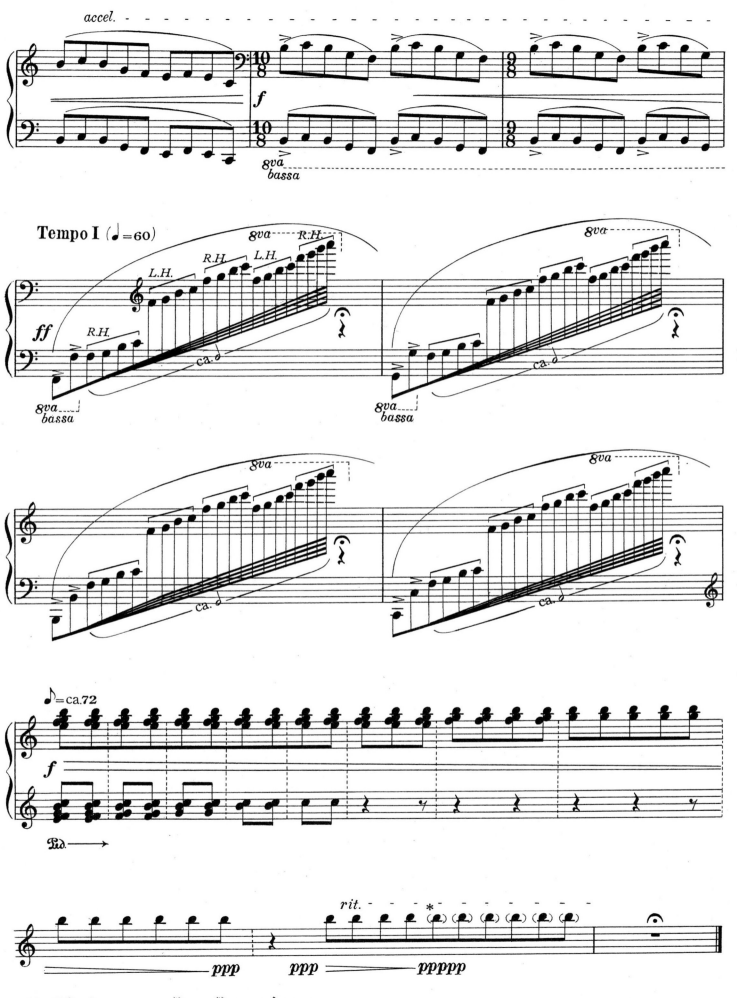

*  (♪) は鍵盤を押すアクションの音のみ。音はもはや聴こえない。
   (♪) means the sound of action to push the key. There is no longer any musical sound to be heard.

# 11
# 風の悲しみ
## Winds in Sorrow
### ＝ドビュッシーへのオマージュ＝
—an Homage to Debussy—

チェレスタのような透明な音色をイメージして下さい。
冒頭の ♫♫♫♫ はペダルを踏んだまま、音階の各音の混ざり合いを
美しく響かせるように。
中間部はグレゴリア聖歌風に。これも余韻を美しく。

Imagine such a transparent tone color as celesta's.
Keep the pedal on during ♫♫♫♫ at the beginning so as to beautifully
reverberate the mixture of each note of the scale.
Play the midsection like a Gregorian chant. Here again take care of the beautiful aftersound.

新実徳英　作曲
Tokuhide Niimi

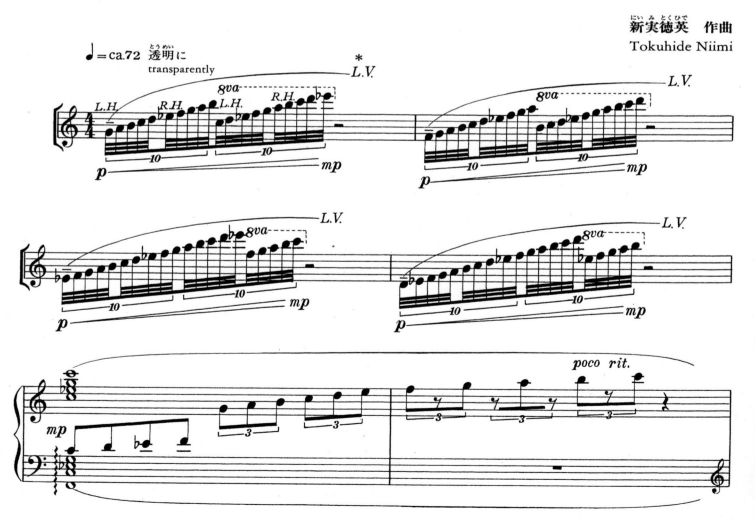

\* *L. V.*＝Laissez Vibrer（35頁参照）。

© Copyright 1992 by edition KAWAI, Tokyo, Japan.
International Copyright Secured, All Rights Reserved.

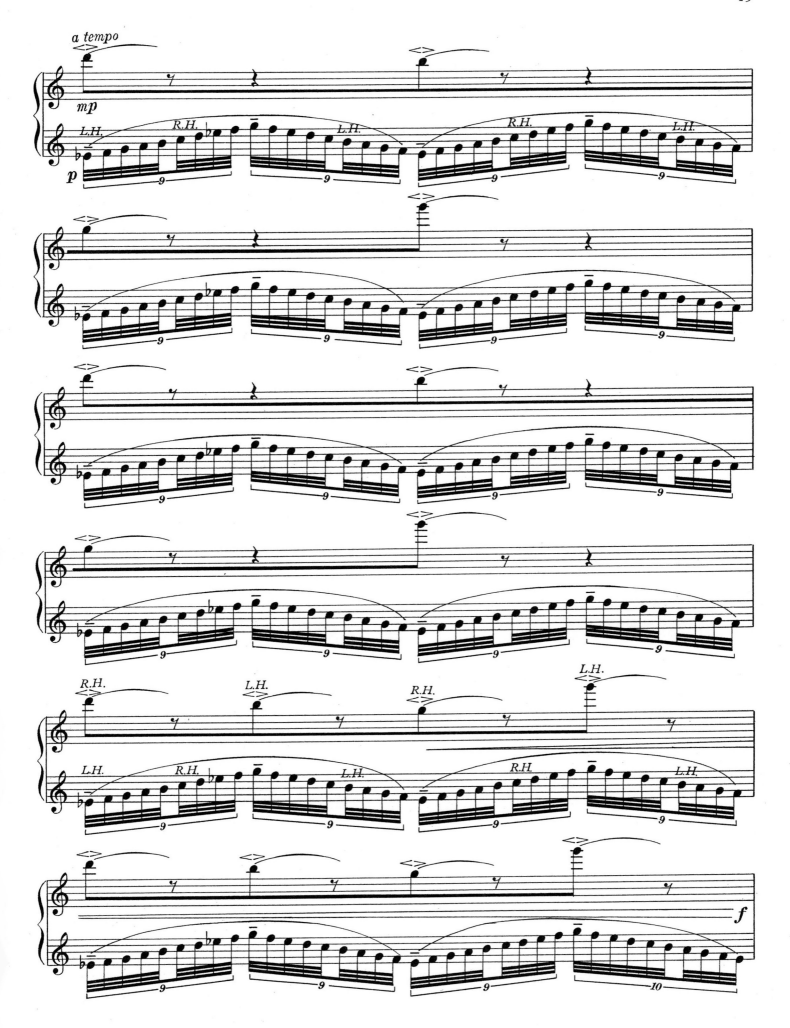

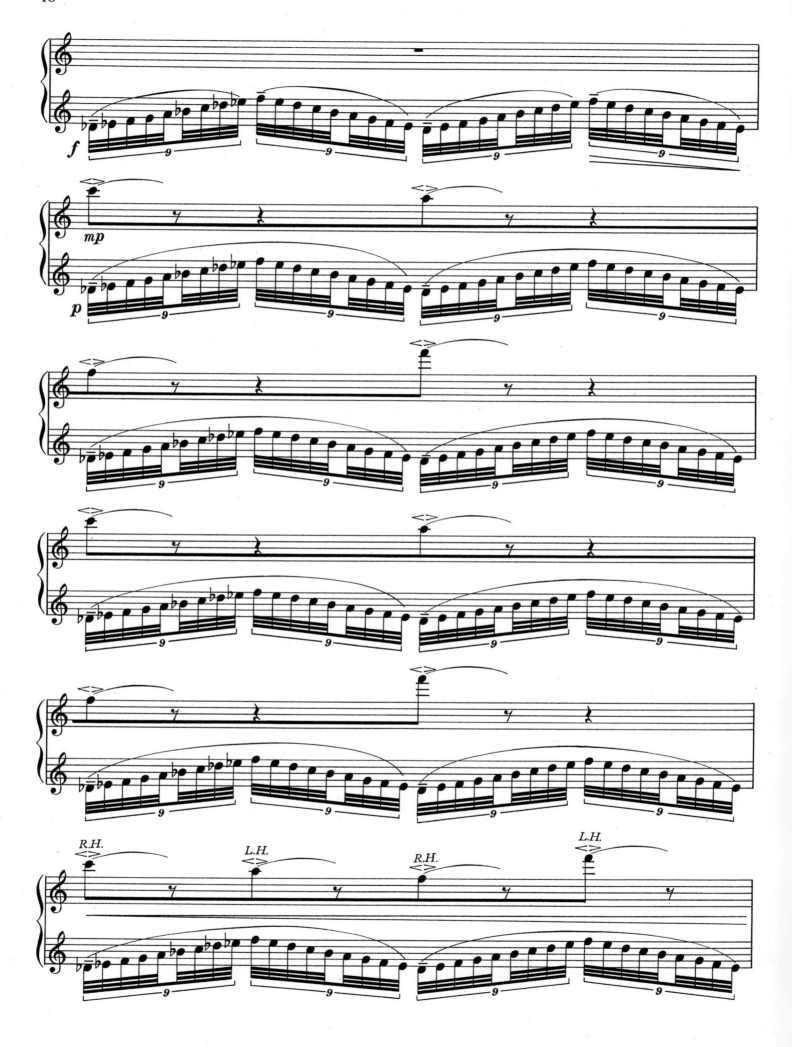

48

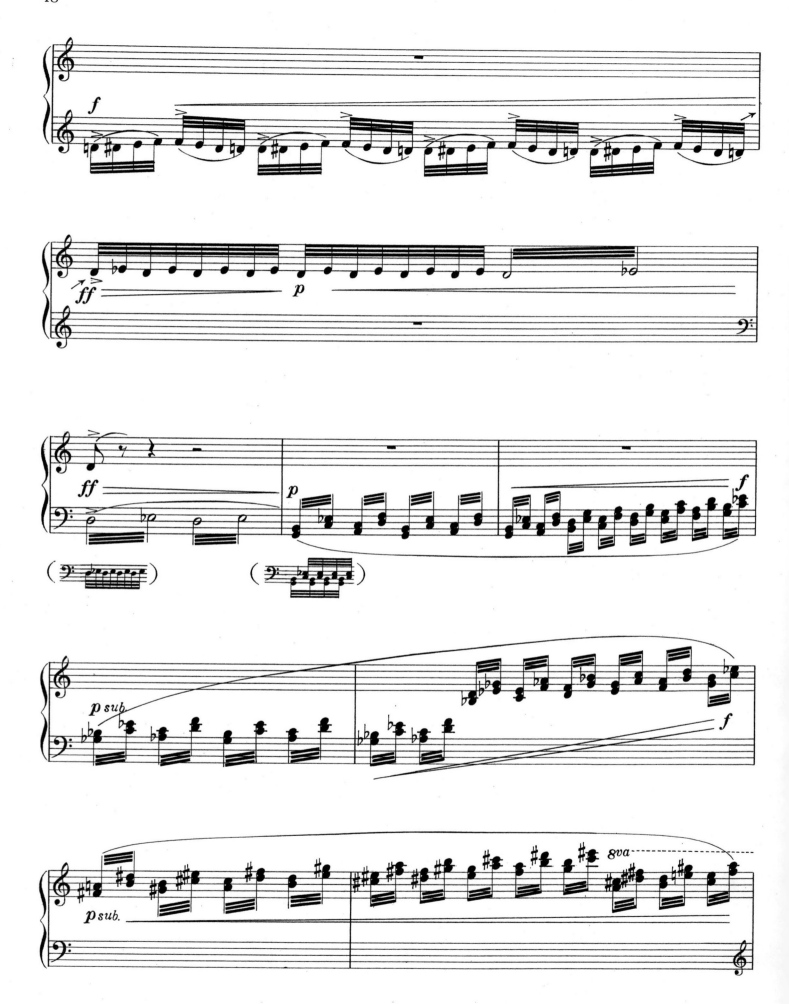

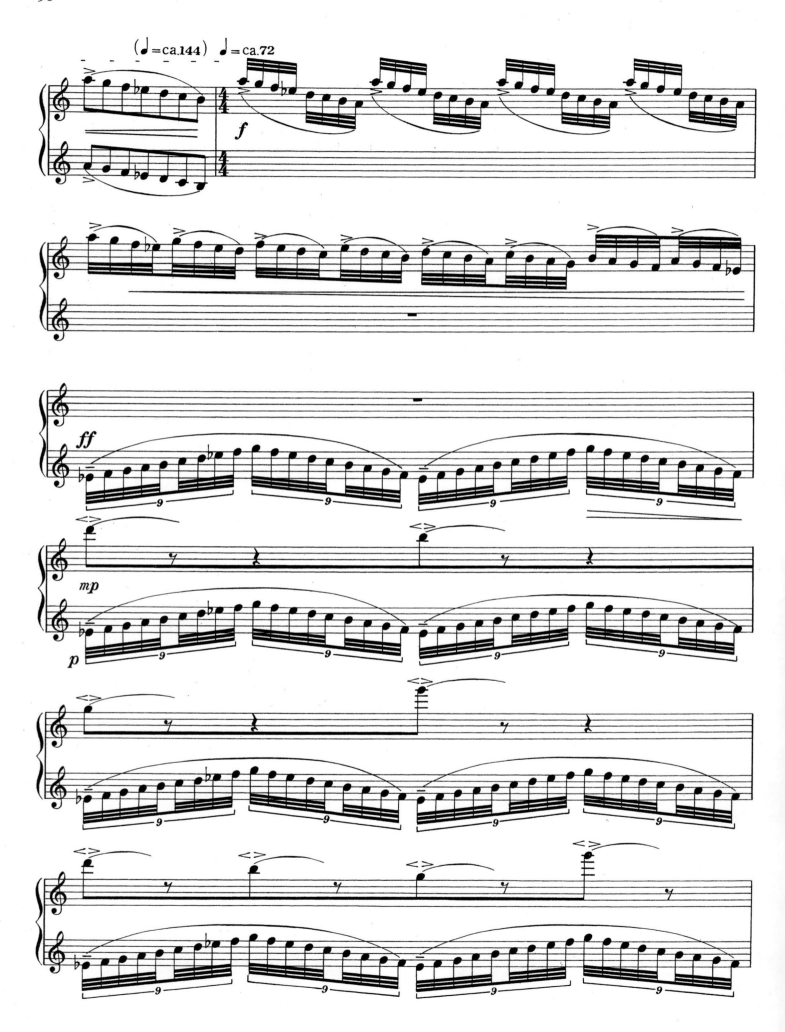

51

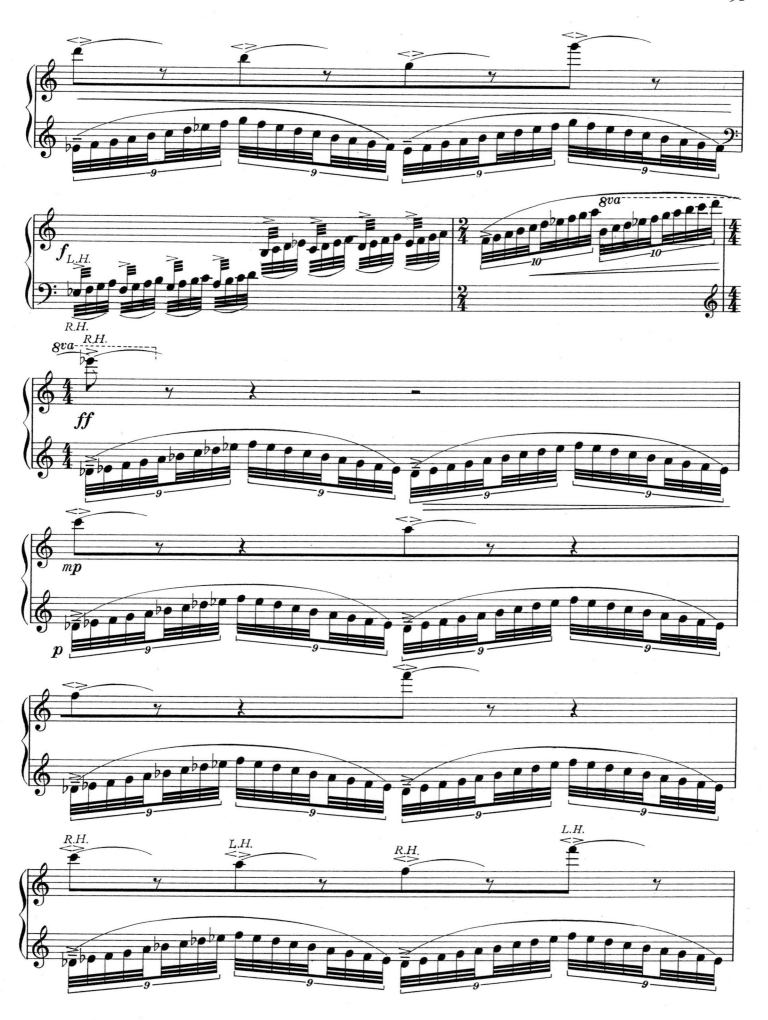

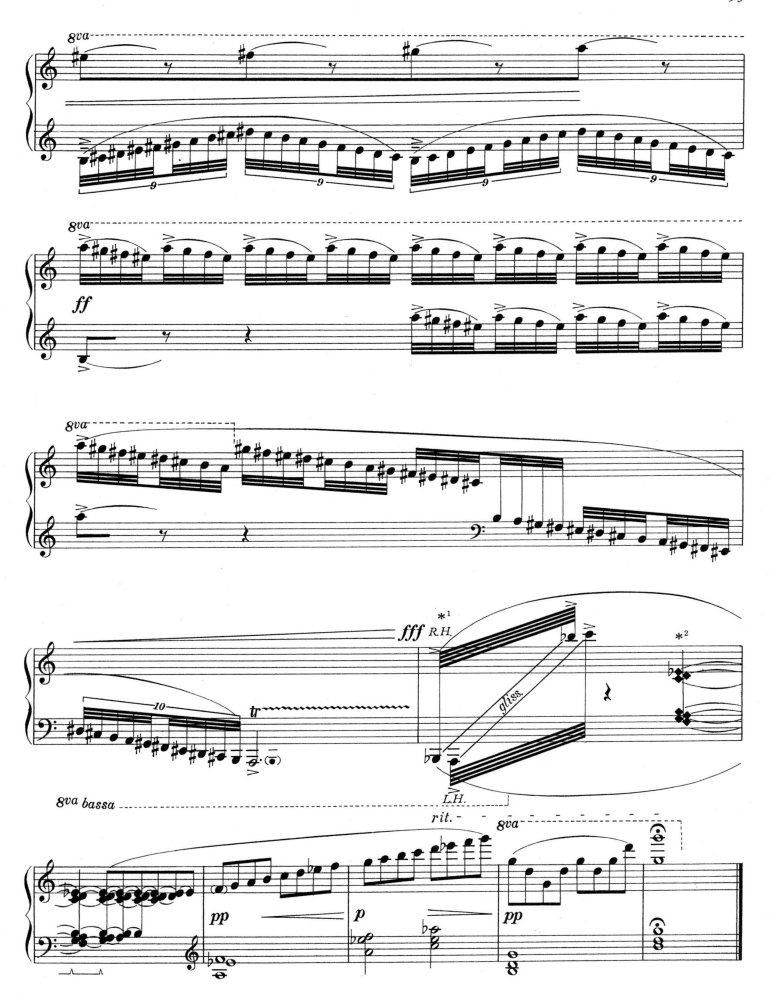

*[1] 右手は黒鍵の，左手は白鍵のグリッサンド。
Glissando on black keys on the right hand and on white keys on the left hand respectively.

*[2] 音の出ぬように押さえる。
Just push the key without any sound.

## 12
### 風は見る……
### The Wind Sees....

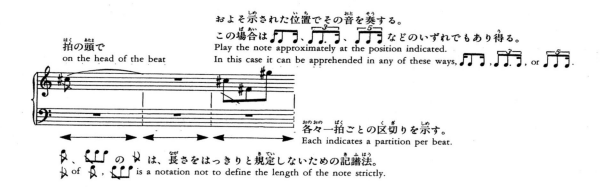

一拍ごとの仕切り線があるだけで、いわゆる拍子はありません。
音の自由な流れを楽しんで下さい。
ドリアの旋法が主体となって作られています。
<≥>のついた音は、やわらかくふくらみのある音で。ペダルは短かく切り過ぎぬように。

There is no what is called time except that it has a partition line per beat.
Find pleasure in the free flow of sound.
This is mainly made up of dorian mode.
The notes with <≥> are to be soft and rich. Do not cut off the pedalling too short.

新実徳英　作曲
Tokuhide Niimi

\* *L. V.* = Laissez Vibrer (35頁参照)。

© Copyright 1992 by edition KAWAI, Tokyo, Japan.
International Copyright Secured, All Rights Reserved.

56

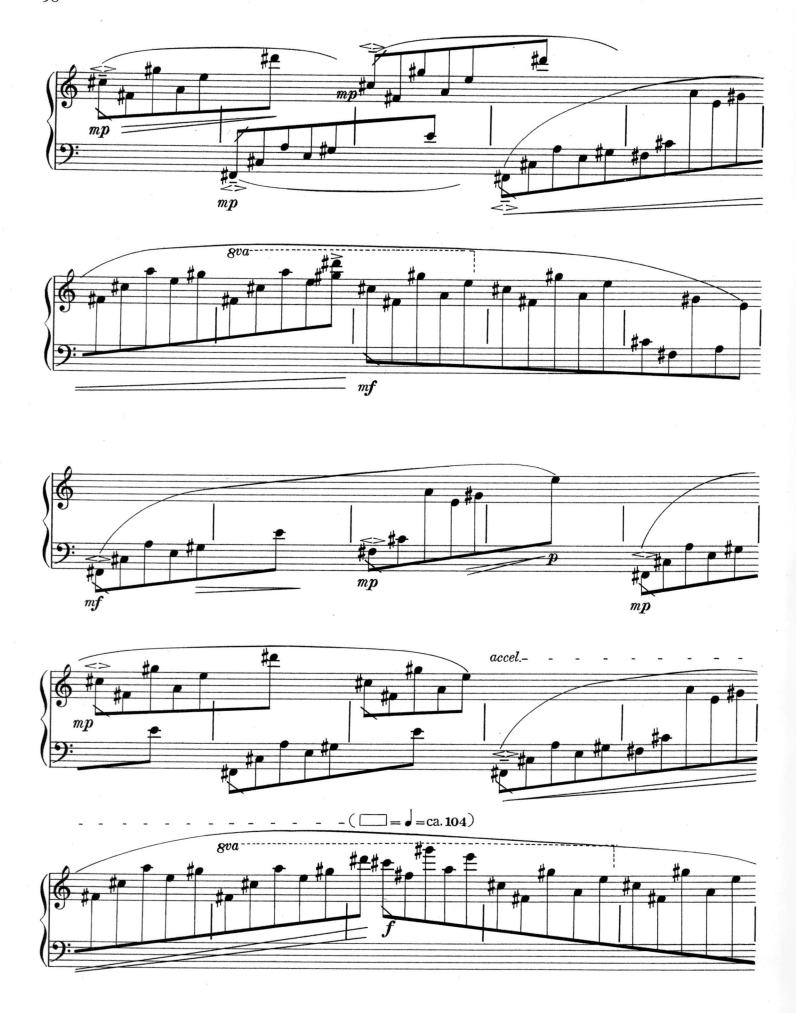

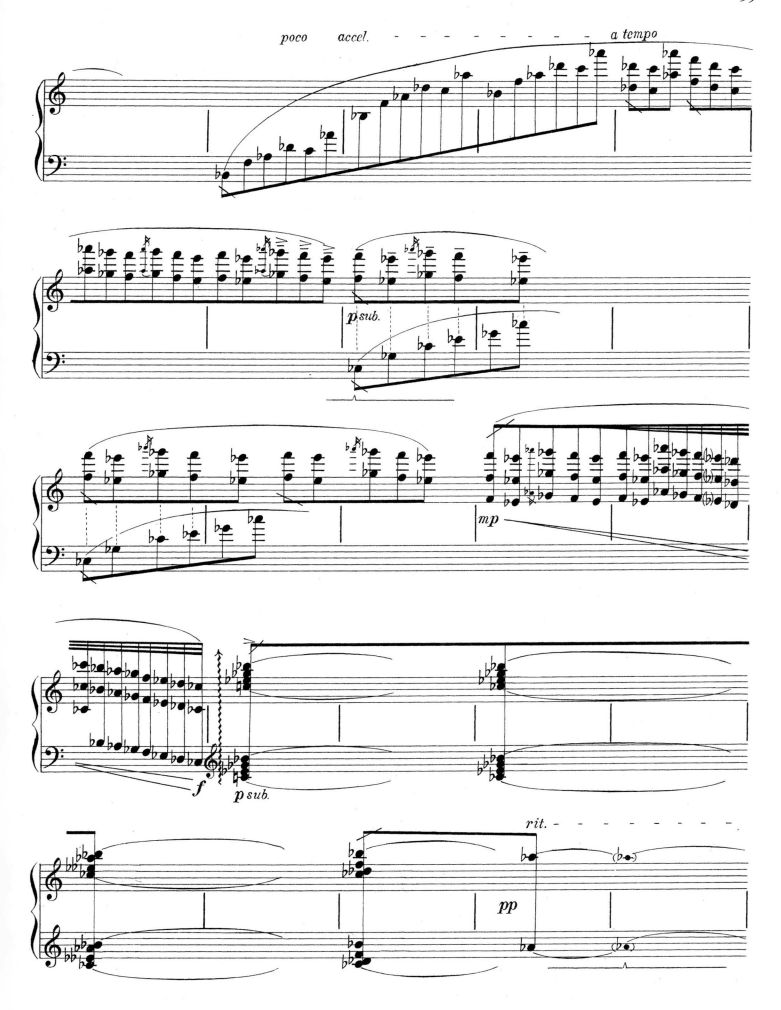

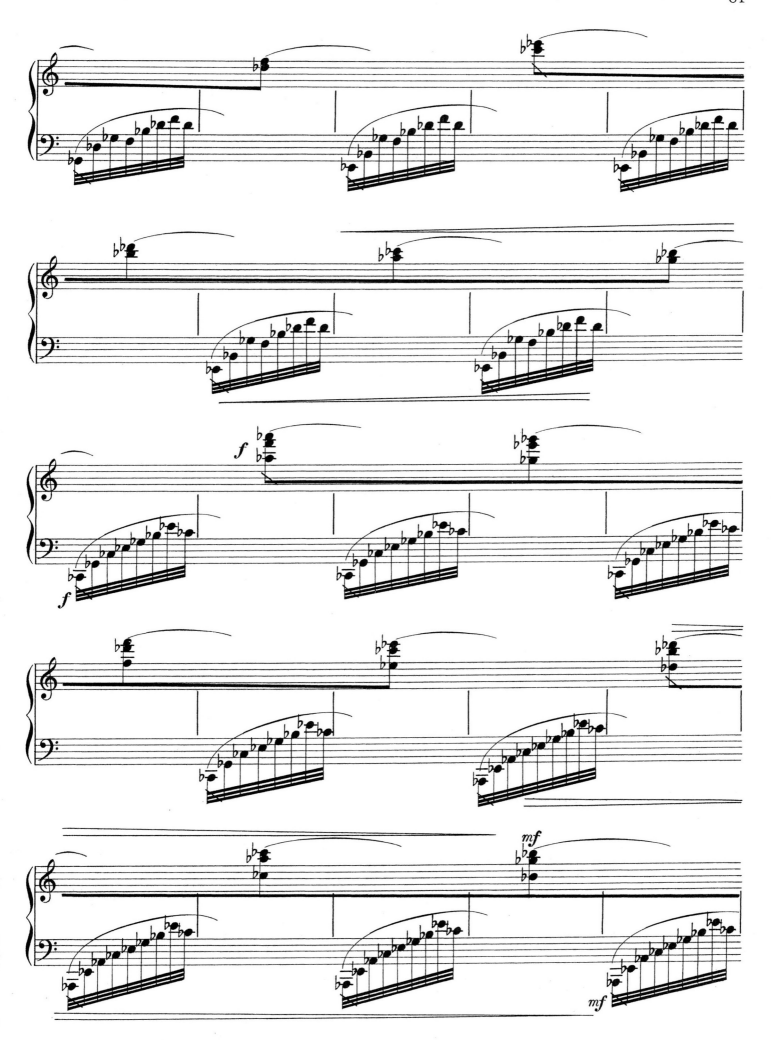

62

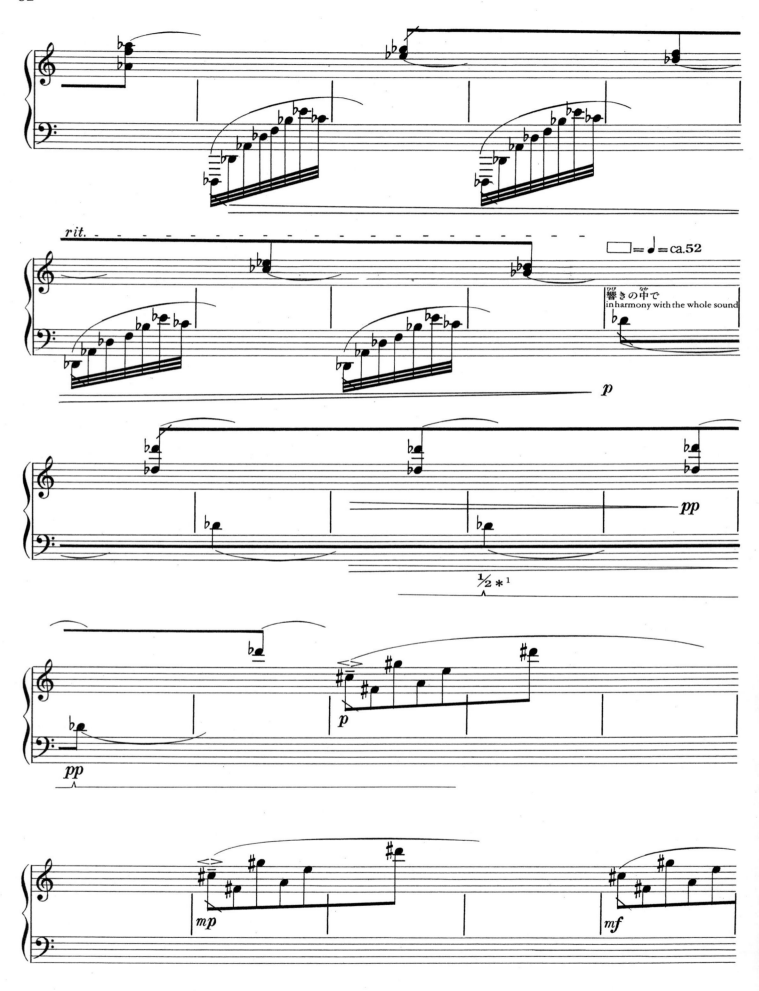

*[1] ½はペダルを半分だけ踏みかえる。
½ here means to shift the pedalling to the halves and keep it on by half.

*[2] 各音の余韻を全て充分に残して。
Leave behind all the aftersound of each note to the fullest extent.

| | こどものためのピアノ曲集<br>**風のプレリュード** | |
|---|---|---|
| 発行日● 1992 年 8 月 1 日　第 1 刷発行 | 作　曲●新実徳英 | |
| 　　　　2025 年 5 月 1 日　第 8 刷発行 | 発行所●カワイ出版（株式会社 全音楽譜出版社 カワイ出版部） | |
| | 〒 161-0034　東京都新宿区上落合 2-13-3 | |
| 表紙絵・イラスト●岩井壽照 | TEL.03-3227-6286　FAX.03-3227-6296 | |
| 表紙デザイン●山本卓美 | 楽譜浄書●ミタニガクフ | |
| 翻訳●前嶋律子 | 写植●フォトタイプ潤 | |
| | 印刷 / 製本●平河工業社 | |

© 1992 by edition KAWAI. Assigned 2017 to Zen-On Music Co., Ltd.

本書よりの転載はお断りします。
落丁・乱丁本はお取り替え致します。
本書のデザインや仕様は予告なく変更される場合がございます。

ISBN978-4-7609-0521-8